How the World Works

Kahran Singh

BookLeaf Publishing

Presentation by *BookLeaf Publishing*

Web: www.bookleafpub.com

E-mail: info@bookleafpub.com

ISBN: 978-93-95621-35-9

First edition 2022

DEDICATION

To our younger selves.

ACKNOWLEDGEMENT

I am so happy that this is in print. It could have never happened without Divya Tak. Divya, you have been such an exciting addition to my life. The roads we have been and the roads we have yet to go!

Thank you also to my partner and cheerleader Gourav Tarafdar, who is always supporting carving out time for poetry. Love you, Gourav.

Thank you also my dear Katie Vogul. You saw me as a poet before I saw myself.

Thank you for your love and support, dear family: Ambika, Rubie, Pradeep, Shankar, Chandan, Bhima, Kesin.

Who are we

We are the joy
that comes so strongly

You wonder

Did this come from within
or is this from without,
The dust of an idle fairy
Or curse gone awry
and bringing such joy

You wonder

Is this the perfect moment
And then remember
Eternity is in this moment
And forever is now.

it's a snack

Did you know
That spiders
Travel with one long
Solitary line of silk
That they leave behind
Whenever they go a-searching
For a new home.

Or perhaps
it's a snack
To eat
On an idle Tuesday
When the markets are closed
And you are left
Wondering
Did I know an existence
Before these routines
I live
Made me one.

Sometimes

3

To touch
in a way
gives remembrance
I don't know
if I can take
Sometimes

warm glows

When I laugh
with you
There is this warm glow
i feel
that comes up from my tummy
and settles in a strange place
behind the lungs
Just there
pleasantly warm
Until I forget to think about it
anymore
And all that's left is a memory
Of something pleasantly warm
On a cold day
Like chocolate
Simmered hot
With a few marshmallows
White clouds of goodness
In a dark brown sea.

Whywasi soalone

In empty shelves
oncei saw

loneliness

It made me miss my friends

the books

Whywasi soalone.
Then I decided
In empty shelves

I would

dream of what could be

and now

I miss my friends

the books

But resent some

A bit

For taking up too much space
with an

over fat cover

or

a cd case

or

other

relics

of

my heart.

your time was long ago.

I came out

In the morning you can listen to the mist. It dies
as it burns, little by little, slow by slow.

If you sit still and don't move your eyes you can
see it fleeing.

It runs from the invading sun, hoping,
wondering,
Thinking maybe today, maybe this day, even if I
don't win, one of us will.

Their kiss is soft and cool on my skin, and tastes
of a color I've never seen.

When I first came out I saw the drops of dew
and wondered — is this? Will this be?

Then their bodies broke together, melded into
ever bigger drops, and I remembered, oh, yes,
this is the ocean, just come to play
 in the air
for a time.

a feather's brush

the light sings to me in the morning
coos, really, a feather's brush against my ears.

drum, drum, drum.

But then it rains and I wonder about the birds

what do they think, when the rain falls without
end, and hunger drives them forth?

What do they think, buffeted by wind and water,
berated flying bodies?

change or die, says the rain.

drum, drum, drum.

soothed though I am by the contortions of these
soft wet bodies on these cold hard surfaces

they drown out the birds.

drum, drum, drum

a landscape

Hello sister
Her white head turns and
I watch her wings
The feathers quiver in the breeze
Behind her,
the boys row
in a feat of strength.
Behind them,
there are the mountains.

an involuntary manslaughter

I watched a butterfly today
It was beautiful and orange
And had a certain way about it
Maybe it was the way it
Fluttered its wings
A daintiful wink
A debutante poised, posed
Ready.
As I passed by
Ensconced in perfect climate
I heard the slight thud
Of a delicate body
Caught in the draft of my passage.

amirite

Is it better to know this is your last goodbye
Mutter words of encouragement
Suggestions of forlorn strength
too little
too late
Paltry nothings to fill
a silence

This time when the silence comes
There will be no escape
No respite on a beach
To mutter words of encouragement
too little
too late
too soon
too gone
The timing is never right until there is no time at
all, amirite?

Nah man maybe it's better

Let the guillotine come in the night
Sharp strokes and sharp blades
Exhaust not my precious store of hope.

inappropriately immodest

Sometimes I smile at myself
(in the mirror)
And wonder
What-must-it-be-like
to be my friend.

But then am caught
(blushing)

And wonder
Why must it feel so
inappropriately immodest
when caught by these thoughts?

jewels

13

I watch my hair
Turn golden
In the reflection of my eyes
I wonder
that this dazzling array
of reds and greens
of browns and oranges
existed
beneath, (or should I say above),
My Nose
and, (fool that I was),

I just went and called it all black.

Eleven

kiss me bitch,

i'm yours

wasn't that the contract we made

under the oak tree

when i let you shoot

and instead of an apple

you split my head.

only it was yours.

ten

is there poetry in anxiety

or does that rush of fear

wonder

awake

(goddamn it is a rush isn't it)

preclude that part of the brain

that stitches together lines and dots

and calls them meaning.

hey you, dead leaf

how come some
lodge themself
so deeply
you can't quite remember
everyone else
or everything,

hey you, dead leaf
you look like a butterfly.

when i'm gone

Sing to me of tomorrow,

oh love

Sing to me of tomorrow,

of pearly gates

and doors held fast.

Mother of pearl is shiny

Until you put your fist through it

And then all it is

is sharp

And there is blood.

five

i'm grateful for my scars
they are unforgettable, see,
and remind me of days long past
whose neighbors are forgotten
lost to miseries of time and toil
and judgement and grief

i'm grateful too to my heart
it beats slow and steady
(higher when i'm excited)

i'm grateful too to my writing
it pulls me in
sometimes
lets me wonder
oh is it? is this? could it be?
could i be?
i wonder.

Xoxo

How lucky am I;
To be surrounded by;
so much love,
We'd have conversations
(about picking and choosing)
whose love,
We'd rather keep.

All that remains

In so far as there is love
There is loss
For no person walks without its shadow
No shadow walks without its name.

-be free my shadow-

Take heed, my captain
This light ahead is too harsh
These shadows will be all that remain.

The world was glad for him

The world was glad for him
for he was a good man.
Man is a term bandied by a few
and good is a term bandied by many
But to be Just
'A good man'
a certain elegance in that.

When your cells stitch together
and another is born
in some remanent
'you'
Some particle or form
I hope they do grace by you.
For grace is something hard to come by
And easy to squander
And yet you had it in spades.

Goodnight, sweet prince.
May your rest be long
May it be quiet
And may you carry burdens no more.

been a while

It's been a while
Since I saw
a cloud perched
a top a hill
Wondering
If anyone could see
How cute it looked
with its hair all peaked
and nose adorned.